JUST A TRACE OF MOON

Also by Ken Fontenot

POETRY
After the Days of Miami
All My Animals and Stars
In a Kingdom of Birds

FICTION
For Mr. Raindrinker

Just a Trace of Moon

Selected Poems
2006 - 2013

By
Ken Fontenot

PINYON PUBLISHING
Montrose, Colorado

Copyright © 2015 by Ken Fontenot

All rights reserved. Except as permitted under the U.S. Copyright Act of 1976, no part of this publication may be reproduced, distributed, or transmitted in any form or by any means, or stored in a database or retrieval system, without the prior written permission of the publisher, except for brief quotations in articles, books, and reviews.

Photograph of Ken Fontenot by Andrew Thomas

Art & Design by Susan Elliott

First Edition: March 2015

Pinyon Publishing
23847 V66 Trail, Montrose, CO 81403
www.pinyon-publishing.com

Library of Congress Control Number: 2015933005
ISBN: 978-1-936671-31-1

Acknowledgments

BORDERLANDS: TEXAS POETRY REVIEW: "All," "In a Bar near Midnight"

MAPLE LEAF RAG III: "Just a Trace of Moon"

MAPLE LEAF RAG IV: "To a Red Leaf"

MAPLE LEAF RAG V: "A Toast"

PINYON REVIEW: "Meditation in Fall," "Something Modern, Something Old," "What About the Birds?," "Next-Door Neighbor," "A Security Job," "It Wants to Stay," "Things Both Practical and Sublime," "Lepidoptera"

PRAIRIE SCHOONER: "Friends, 1956"

REFLECTIONS, AUSTIN POETRY SOCIETY, 2009: "Where I Want to Groan Is Green—Saturday"

TEXAS OBSERVER: "Prerequisites"

"Friends, 1956" also appeared on Poetry Daily, September 29, 2009.

I would also like to express my gratitude to my critique group in Austin for their good counsel. They are: Kath Anderson, Bob Ayres, Marcy Buffington, Lynn Gilbert, Judith Infante, André Jordan, and Frances Schenkkan.

For Christine and Jacques Leche

Contents

I

Something Modern, Something Old 3
Meditation in Fall. 4
What About the Birds? 5
Next-Door Neighbor 6
A Security Job 7
Friends, 1956. 8
That Is Its Way 9
Just a Trace of Moon 10
A Toast. 11
All 12
In a Bar Near Midnight 13
It Wants to Stay 14
A Beat 15
I Recall Watching John Larroquette on an Episode of
    "Night Court." 16
Johannes. 17
Katrina, Still Uncertain in the Gulf But Already a
    Category 4 Storm 18

II

Back Then 21
1960. 22
Window View 23
To a Red Leaf. 24
To a Pigeon 25
Winter. 26
Where I Want to Groan Is Green—Saturday 27
After a PBS Special I Gaze out the Window 28
This Is No Way to Love Things. 29
More Than Water. 30
Your Life Here During the Siege of Vietnam 31
An Egg on the Ground. 32
How the Dark Arrives 33
Things Both Practical and Sublime. 34
An Imagined Song 35
The Entertainers' Virtue, 1962 36
Rhetorical Question. 37
Pepe Romero Plays Boccherini 38

III

Lepidoptera 41
You Wonder Why 42
A Young Woman 43
The Children Believe Spring 44
Bestiary 45
Poem Meant to Satisfy Horace's *Ars Poetica* as to What Literature Should Do 46
The Brilliance and the Wisdom 47
The Clouds over Two Smaller Shapes 48
Concert 49
Young in Acadia Parish 50
The Ghosts of the Books in the Library 51
The Octogenarian Who Still Likes Sinatra 52
Boys, Beauty, Rattlesnakes 53
Falstaff 54
Andante 55

IV

February 14th	59
12 Dalton Road	60
Wednesday Only in Some of Our Minds	61
The Compressed Matter of Youth	62
Like Judy Garland, One of the Gumm Sisters	63
Happy Birthday	64
Who Abets War? Who Does Not?	65
Is He Still Alive?	66
He Who Leaves His Money in Mutual Funds	67
For Daniel	68
Prerequisites	69

I

SOMETHING MODERN, SOMETHING OLD

The songs of my time insist we listen attentively.
Take Fleetwood Mac. They incite, almost all melody,
which is the pie's filling, the alcohol in a mixed
        drink.
O Stevie Nicks! You carry your instrument around
in your throat. You walk with it, sleep with it.
It lives inside you, moves inside you like
        your heart.
"Sara" and "Gypsy" emerge resembling a husky Edith Piaf,
so tender, so helpless is your loneliness.
And a kind of quiet grief defines these limits.

But in my more somber moods I prefer Beethoven.
Surely even his enemies couldn't remove his ethos,
one of an Apollonian-and-Dionysian-bold majesty.
If only Nietzsche had been able to shake his hand!
If only Germany had been able to shake
        the world's hand!

I wish I had a nickel for each prickle I've
felt along my neck, as music carried along
the best of my spirit, always warm, always golden.

MEDITATION IN FALL

1.
Day emerges from a dull grayness,
one the children can't know in their sleep.
I could say there are birds,
but there are none, not now anyway.
What cool mornings in fall,
what stamina the unheard from possess.
I'm moving from expectation into awe.
That's how the first people behaved, I think.
Or take desire. It should be forgotten
until a real need demands it.

2.
Ah, does anyone know where the bees live?
I want to find them, see how
contagious their patience is.
Lacking that, however,
I won't underestimate the trees,
won't believe in a sad nothingness the dogs
of the night seem to howl at the moon.

3.
Desire and power are blood brothers.
So the quick bird escapes the quick cat.
Just barely this time. As for the next,
who can predict? Whose redemption:
safe, assured, and benevolent as ever.

WHAT ABOUT THE BIRDS?

Thunderstorms. Lightning so close
the thought of it striking is unsettling.
Remember the golfers who sought shelter
beneath trees in weather like this?
It was their last, heartbreaking game.
Then we have the story of a blind man
struck by lightning. He could see again!
And he lived to tell everyone about it.

It's not easy to view ourselves as lab mice
in evolution's great experiment. In fact,
this is just one lull in the earth's stormy history.
But go ahead: take another sip of wine
and expect not catastrophe, but giddiness.
Expect to be brilliant about brilliance.
Let the brain have its own odd say.
At times it will declare its fate a mistrial anyway.

As for the sparrows these days, they're doing
just fine. Talkative as ever and feisty to boot.

NEXT-DOOR NEIGHBOR

Summer in the grass and he taps his nails
against the desk. Forget the heat. The light
made a Loretta Young entrance, he having
pushed aside the curtains of his old age.
Still drumming out a tune with his fingers,
he recalls what mattered: a farm from which
his father sent him to New Orleans, a wife
whose liver quit in deepest winter, one child.

The bodies he entered, the wishes he began with:
neither as important as the patina of wisdom
that formed across his forehead over the years.
Many of his interests arrived with one full moon
or another. And he chopped hardwood. He pulled weeds.
Once, coming home from a bar, he fell asleep
at the wheel and crashed through a store window.

But exactly where has his good luck taken him?
Over a hill, under a bridge of comings and goings,
beyond cities and their great souls, across deserts
where water was illusory and sand a reminder,
through mountains resembling women's breasts.

Even now he forecasts his days like tomorrow's weather.
Thumbs up for this year's tomatoes, thumbs up for
getting a new pet, thumbs down for the life of his Ford.

A SECURITY JOB

In the morning I relieve him.
He's had a long night.
Watching monitors. Entertaining silence
with his own lasting silence.
As usual the sun came up. I am here.
I discover nothing new about this building
whose presence, now on Sunday,
ghosts inhabit. The past confronts me.
Suddenly I am a boy, six,
swimming at a place called
the Kinder Pump in Kinder, Louisiana,
a big rice pump
which pushed hundreds of gallons per minute.
We kids like to stand under it.
Feel the heavy water
as if it were a waterfall in the mountains.
But there are no mountains. Only flat land.
And pine trees. Last year a baby copperhead
bit my cousin Horace. Who lived through it.
Who lives even now as I write this.
Dear reader, we were meant to swim.
Just the presence of the past
either confounds us or elates us.
Let me have this pleasant moment
all to myself.

FRIENDS, 1956

We were pure energy without wisdom.
We were the embarrassment of short pants
and short hair. We were dust
creased in the neck, fingers around a baseball bat.
We were the lovers of lost time,
and we spent much of it ourselves.
We were smokers in hiding,
stalled cars miles from home.
We were white socks with a brown suit.
We were all sweat in our coats,
always a nickel short,
ten steps ahead.
We could have swum in clear rivers.
We could have swum in deep lakes.
We could have sung songs to the trees.
We had green knees forever.
We sulked ten steps behind.
We ran our dogs to the bone.

THAT IS ITS WAY

We must try to be as if always balanced on a bicycle
since all of nature does so in spite of our own
meager attempts. Look at birds perfectly
balanced on the wires. At ants
bearing many times their ant-weight. Hawks
on extended wings. Dolphins in exact leaps.
The trees anchored. The grass whole. The hummingbird
      steady.
Only we are not secure with the cargo of irretrievable loss
and the bad days of the spirit and the desire unreturned
      by the Wished For.
Beloveds, don't you think it is time to make peace
so that, if indeed we part, the air will be less tense
around us? Less apt to choke us with anger?

Already there are signs of winter in the old mind.
Those of us, whose parents have just passed
into another realm of transformation, we need to find a way
to be our own parents now, just as they did for *theirs*.
When Goethe said, "Two souls live in me," he must have
meant the angelic and the demoniac. And he
lived the balance; he could take both into old age.

But the snake sheds its skin. That is its way. There is
      no other.

JUST A TRACE OF MOON

A bear was walking in the snow of your dreams.
This was far north, the bear perfectly white.

Powerful, a cub on each side, she seemed
determined the day would not be wasted.

You awaken; the memory of bear already begins
to vanish. You sigh, quite pleased

with the TV pictures from your sleep.
Were you the bear, restless, hungry, befriended?

Not snow, but greenery surrounds your house.
Midsummer. That word sticks in your mind.

"Midsummer," for which everything appears prepared.
Just a trace of moon. The bees go on with their work.

The cat yawns and stretches. What usefulness,
what galactic importance can the quotidian have?

Don't think, since the air is fully placid,
you'll escape loss like the survivor of a train wreck.

Your family photos might be ruined in a flood.
A driver might run a light, leaving you paralyzed.

Yet take heart: the horse you ride today may not
throw you, but will make you tremble.

A TOAST

In the coffeehouse I try to read.
Students to my left are discussing

courtroom procedures for, maybe, Legal Issues 221.
Everybody except me has an Apple laptop.

The music—I believe it's Miles—
no words, no blatant distraction.

The counter help been getting their tips?
Open and close a phone. Go ahead.

In my youth—not theirs—I couldn't
do this. If the Mexican poet in translation

were here, what would he make of it all?
Something about coffee. How it encourages

the tongue, or doesn't, and harms our sleep
instead. Let's stay up all night!

Let's have a few beers too. A toast to Miles.
A toast to the man without money even for the bus.

ALL

Planetary moods—distant and miniscule—
leave us wanting even more than astronomy.
Astonishment, sure, sometimes when
our thoughts are not on the pot
we left boiling, and have to rush back.
So the quotidian means a re-evaluation.
Should the dog be bathed again today?
Should our simple fears be sorted out?
Should the most, the very most of love
be looked at squarely in the face?

Always the newness. Always the starting over.
Always the nostalgia for our best years.

And then the quickness of children,
how their feet are agile as their minds.

And then the way back, the putting up,
the seamless cloth where all is well.

IN A BAR NEAR MIDNIGHT

A beautiful girl says *hello*.
He wonders why. He smiles
for the first time in months.
What he needs to know:
is there someone in her life?
No. Better not to know.
Not now anyway. Suddenly
he feels up to a short lecture.
"Ever read Goethe?" he asks.
Who? "Goethe, the German genius
who lived from 1749 to 1832."
Sorry. "His life was a precious stone.
In his dreams all the women
in town knocked on his door.
Once Napoleon himself took
the time to look him up.
He wrote so awfully much
it'd take years to read him.
And he never even found anyone
he could put a wedding ring on.
But as an old man he lived
with a girl, 19, Christiane Vulpius
who bore him a son.
In world literature only
Shakespeare and Dante can compare.
Wouldn't you like to meet
a writer as talented, as godly?
(You know, the gods chose him.)
Wouldn't you like to remain
in the company of someone like him?"
No, not really, I just need a light.

IT WANTS TO STAY

We breathe
the almost nothingness of dust
which survives us all.

Its reappearance trick
takes its time, arriving finally
as a guest unannounced.

Just run your finger
over the coffee table.

A mote of dust
contains a mote of truth:

it has the last laugh.

A BEAT

The artifice in many symphonies
is to rev the music up
as if *this* were the forceful closure.
It's a trick, a tease, a kind of suspense,
and the symphony does *not* end here—
you've been fooled—
but proceeds calmly, or moderately,
or violently onward.
Beethoven likes it. So does Mahler,
especially in his First, the *Titan*.

The classical station on the radio.
I scrub the pot. Blackened
through my forgetting it. I make my own
little symphony out of scraping.
Rhythm. No melody except humming.
Percussive. A beat of sorts.

I still have no idea when I'll
be ready to proceed calmly,
or moderately, or violently onward.

I RECALL WATCHING JOHN LARROQUETTE ON AN EPISODE OF "NIGHT COURT."

What I felt for you was what undid
Othello and tormented Iago.
Ah, it was only for a short while, then the feeling—
from that double kingdom—passed.

Now I say let's drink to failure
for a change. Let's drink to those who gave
their best swings but kept striking out.

Never mind you were always the ham,
always the incorrigible skirt chaser,
the one with the timing.
Twenty years before, in high school,
we acted together in another court:
"Trial by Jury" from Gilbert and Sullivan.

Who would have guessed you'd later wear
the laurels: not one, or two,
but four Emmys all in a row.
How long, how long until I knew for sure:
praise given to you does not mean
praise taken from me?

JOHANNES

Brahms' "Tragic Overture" and his "Academic Festival
Overture." Both written the same summer.

The first somber, opaque. The other joyous, clear.
He needed both at once to be truthful to himself.

He needed music he could balance on like a tightrope.
In every countryside he felt melodies so plentiful

he could step on them. But melody was only a fraction
of music. The rest: being a magician every day.

The longer he lived, the more he just composed to get by.
His cancer of the liver—his father's cancer too.

For love he almost always relied on prostitutes.
A penchant as natural as his perfect pitch.

No operas from him, nor symphonies longer than
those of Mahler and Bruckner at their greatest.

You might look at the last photo of him
and think (rightly so in many ways)—a bear not dancing.

KATRINA, STILL UNCERTAIN IN THE GULF BUT ALREADY A CATEGORY 4 STORM

We know the eye. How calm it is.
Being like the Buddha, center of all centers.
The rest: just the troublesome winds of desire.
Wet wind, wet kisses—what's the difference?

Spare the coast. Return to the ocean where you are
comfortable churning. Open water, after all,
is nothing to you. Your birthplace southeast
of the Bahamas, you need some sea space to revel in.
What have we done to make you seek us out?
What provoked the gods to send you, O harbinger
       of maybe harder days to come?

II

BACK THEN

On forms I filled out as a kid I wrote
"housewife" or "homemaker" as my mother's
         occupation.
She signed my report cards Mrs. W. P. Fontenot
in her beautiful script, something she
must have used a lot in high school,
which is as far as she went, being a Cajun
country girl for whom college wasn't even
an option. During the Second World War
she crisscrossed the country with Western Union.
She teletyped her way into marriage and 1946.

Who got her drunk for her toothache? Who later made
her iced tea, she feeling too bad to make it herself?
I know it was my father. I know he would
have fought the whole terrible War just for her.

1960

The school year ended too slowly
for most: the summer made winter
just another nuisance, another dull forecast.
And how the young love June, July, August!
Each grows into summer like fruit.

Not even bare feet on the hot cement
of the swimming pool's edges discourage them.
Games below the surface—mimicking Lloyd Bridges
in "Sea Hunt"—make up for the pain
of a belly bust off the high board.
Trained in mouth-to-mouth,
the lifeguard on his tall throne
gets funny-eyed stares from teenage girls.

No one will drown here. No one will
mind the chlorine, strong as a double
martini, or the lifeguard, blowing
his whistle at horseplay all summer long.

WINDOW VIEW

Outside, a building behind this bare tree.
The sky behind that one. A tiny sun
in a car's rear window. No blossoms
anywhere except indoors in a vase!

Lucky for all there are flower shops
remaining free from winter.

Lilies light the room. They're calla lilies,
a large white spathe around a yellow spadix.
Two people hang from their chairs, arms
over the chair backs. A party soon.
Not everyone is here yet. A birthday.
And what emptiness when everyone is gone.
Only the lilies then—

TO A RED LEAF

The months turn into eternities,
but looking back it all happened so fast.
My first success riding a bicycle.
My first time driving a car.
My first love, lost irretrievably.
Learning how to write a poem.
A biology final for which I got an A.
The death of my parents.
And now I'm my own parent.
More stars make the biggest difference.
I'm where soul and spirit intersect.
I'm wherever Ceres has saddened.

Cracks are for the light to push through.
Leaves are there to surrender to autumn.
A red leaf is a thing of beauty.
Even though, or especially because, it's vanishing.

TO A PIGEON

Autonomous beast, where—no—how
can I gain your silences? In my own low
soarings, in my own pecking at life's motes?
Your throat and neck an oil slick in color.
Common, mostly docile you are, and not burdened
by what time leaves to the mind: the open end
of existence. Can we be content if we
have not a thing to think about? I ask you,
O bobbing, ashen bearer of much apathy.

WINTER

I don't think the cotton quilt
the aircraft glides over
should be enjoyed any other way
than on our bed.

For there we need a certain warmth
on a cold day and an even colder night.
And what's to say about being cloud-tender
in general, especially toward a beloved?

Especially when the hard nights
with moon are not always tender
toward us.   So let's fly away together
and relearn the tenderness of clouds,
how once long ago only the angels
could see whatever it is we see now.

WHERE I WANT TO GROAN IS GREEN—SATURDAY

A college boy, I stumble into the bathroom
after an all-nighter. Whiskey takes its toll.
Heaving over the toilet—shadowing the green tile
Mom left spotless—I say I won't do it again,
but I will. Half an hour from now,
I must be at the butcher shop, ready for work.
I am so young I can manage, not without regret.

By seven I'm about to cut up Mrs. Schmidt's chicken.
My boss grabs my chin, stares into my eyes.
"Be careful, boy, don't wantcha
bleedin' all over my good saw."

My stomach feels like a beehive.
And I'm in for a very long day,
only to step out of the shop under the sky
and see the tiny lights already on, the ones
I'll see until the earth becomes my equal.

AFTER A PBS SPECIAL I GAZE OUT THE WINDOW

What else can you do, old lion?
The pack of hyenas will only steal
your fresh kill. What else can you do,
dingy grackle, who must have lost
claw and tail to a fight? A rival
will only take your crumbs away.

Today the moon will be almost pale
like someone frightened from behind.

So. Being rueful also belongs to the rain.
It shall have its soaking wet discontent—
a best man, his car top down;
mother and child, between stores.
And for those like them, the fewer, the better.

THIS IS NO WAY
TO LOVE THINGS

Irish potato, I love the color
of your skin, as if tanned underground.
Yes, to be like you with so many eyes
because I just want to see better.
Eyes even in the back of your head.
Look: the farmer digging in the soil,
his son playing behind him, the potato goddess,
a picture of her in the boy's clear imagination.

Now it's after supper—potato soup.
Ah, this is no way to love things;
to go to bed at seven on a Saturday night.
But thus it happens to a sleepyhead.

No. I guess I'll watch the sky awhile
on this clear night. I'll view
the objects in my room, my dreams.
And think how Georgia O'Keeffe took
a long time to see what she most believed in.

MORE THAN WATER

In every language people look skyward
and see things translatable.
What for one is *le ciel*
is for another *der Himmel.*
O these words are loaded with sky-feelings.
There where clouds do a great job
by simply being themselves.
In any case, our skin tingles,
sensing something greater than skin.

Ah, adding the soul to the body,
do we get two or one?
I must ask because at this very minute
a bird is pecking out of its egg,
each of which calls to mind
the great transformation
of a nature gone berserk in spring.

And nothing will stop the golden eagles
from making a mess of some rabbit's flesh.
Goodbye, soul-bearing rabbit,
you were just one among many like you.
Goodbye. Goodbye. Even more than water
is blood the bird of prey's desire,
it who saves none for no one, except fledglings.

YOUR LIFE HERE DURING THE SIEGE OF VIETNAM

(Upstairs from you a man blows his nose.
A stray dog, passing outside, pricks its ears—
we can't move ours and must settle for
whatever location we're in to hear anything.)

The dog, a mixed breed, resembles
the one you lost forty years ago.
You walked the sidewalks with Bert,
rode your bike with him running behind.
It was he you kept asking neighbors about,
kept putting up signs for (offering a modest reward).

Even had you found him, even had
he come home for good, there would have
still been that small pain of separation,
that brief doing without, which, like your
loving, losing, and having someone again,
would have burned deeply and for a long time.

AN EGG ON THE GROUND

All mockingbirds wear the same uniform,
though none belong to any military.
Rather they belong to what the eyes
gladly give the brain. And they run
in spurts and stops, balance on thin things—
metal signs, barbed wire—their tails
keeping them upright. This spring,
outside the house, I see a pair
has lost an egg to the ground.
A haphazard carelessness? I don't know.
I only know another life in oblivion.

HOW THE DARK ARRIVES

The thunder knows only one word (that's loud),
but it's enough to warn us the rain is coming.
And thus if I can't be outside, I can be home
listening to Beethoven, whose music runs toward
a lover with open arms, or shuffles its feet, or is
so sad as to leave two drops stuck to my cheeks,
especially the *andante con moto* movement of
the "Appassionata." Otherwise light pools in the window.
Dim light because the clouds are dark and content
to keep their enthusiasm for light at a minimum.

No, I won't go to sleep, bad weather, tempting
though it might be. Instead, I'll pick my way through
a song on the guitar, whose strings are not "swords"
in the "heart," as Lorca wrote, but exclamation points
announcing the beginning of partitas by Bach.
In this way the dark arrives fresh and without fear.
Don't take it too seriously. It is merely beautiful.

THINGS BOTH PRACTICAL
AND SUBLIME

When months pass like weeks, one can admit
to being thoroughly involved. For schoolchildren
it may have been the summer. For hunters
it may have been the hunting season.

But time ceases when we cease, and we
live our immortality in oblivion. More we
can't say, except the world knows very well
what it's doing, just as the snail plods in triumph.

I wanted to have a distinct plan, yet it changed
as I changed. Even the pines were insightful.
And the cows returned to the barn in their slow way.

The best we can bargain for is authenticity
and gratitude (even more than love?),
for the cow is grateful to the grass, each
showing its true self. So remind me to serve up
a meal of life, the main course of which is grace.

AN IMAGINED SONG

To think of scat singing is to think
of Ella Fitzgerald, though it may be
difficult to name the original, the first.
Perhaps if I consulted Giddins' *Visions
of Jazz*, I'd find my answer. Ah, it
doesn't matter. Listening to Ella suffices.
Just as it matters not who played
the first instrument, or who kissed first,
the entire life being the most important,
so that death arrives none too soon nor
none too late, but rather with a song
on someone's lips, somewhere and somehow.

THE ENTERTAINERS' VIRTUE, 1962

Late, two guests enter the church the light also enters.
Their faces are like the afterlight of some flash bulb.
One recognizes them only when the heavy door closes.
Now everyone is seated.
                              Weddings can be so solemn.
But in the reveries of bride and groom—not the moment
at hand, rather the moment they'll be together alone.
This—even in the parents' minds, they who, lacking
conclusiveness, are happy and sad at the same time.

Even the musicians at the wedding gala are happy
and sad. Although everyone loves their music, one
band member drowned, a week ago, in a boating accident.
Hiding their sorrow well, their virtue is courage.
Their virtue, hard-won and simple, rivals the stars'.

RHETORICAL QUESTION

Avoiding solipsism, I make time for others.
My dog's bark, then, seems a bit more lively.
Ten years in my yard, he has
a baby's tenderness. If only the world saw him
as a hedonic beast, which he just might be
given his habit of rolling over, so anyone
can rub his belly. I don't even mind
that he'd never make a good watchdog.
What's closer to the truth than a mix, life givers?

PEPE ROMERO PLAYS BOCCHERINI

Shoo, thunderclouds. Leave me in peace.
Already my ears are ringing with applause—
that's what I expect from an evening
of fancy guitar fretwork. Practice, and the mind
starts filling up with knowledge, the way
a needle fills up with blood, the phlebotomist
having poked around enough to put you out of sorts.
Will I mesmerize the audience or just entertain?
My fingers knead the strings. The Fandango
Guitar Quintet needs precisely something special.
Otherwise I wouldn't even attempt it. Mostly,
though, I would have wanted Boccherini's dates:
1743-1805. Was it a great time to be alive?
Of course, the music itself seems to say so.

III

LEPIDOPTERA

Chess and my opponent thought:
a questionable move on his part.
I've made a lot of questionable moves,
many of which I'd almost gladly
take back. But the view from here
suffices. Only seven years, then retirement,
though I'll not retire to some rocking chair.
The job no more taxing than a sinecure.
My co-workers: most always ready for a laugh.
A way to pass the time. The pay not bad.
Am able to see a doctor when I need to.
Others with the onus of no health insurance.
I know. Once ashamed to even go
to the emergency room and its dear price.

Above my desk: species of butterflies,
each with a unique color, each precious.
This is what we wish—to be like them.

YOU WONDER WHY

The one life of a book is confirmed by all
the other books on the shelf. Your life confirms
mine. We stand alone and together simultaneously.
And you wonder why there is always trouble?
Jane Goodall saw how even chimps can kill their kind.
But let's forget about murder for the moment.
Let's observe how much silence might exist. Between
two trees in a forest. Between the earth and the moon.
Ah, the patience of wildflowers in the wind's presence.
They do not say: "Get out and don't come back!"
They do not bore us with a lot of literal talk.
There is only one soul to be in awe of—the world's.

A YOUNG WOMAN

Anne told herself she was no longer
learning anything. But today she learned
how choosing what to eat would help her lose weight.
And yesterday she learned of beauty
in how mosquitoes bounce along the air.
So she gave herself not enough credit
like her father and his father who drank too much.
Moody, she told the blackbird, "Just count the stars."
Be my love, tender moon, she thought, though
her true love, Bill, would appear in less
than a year. The seasons would change without
her really sensing it, her job was so demanding.
She could not help recall what her mother said:
"Few women avoid their reflections. Few women
mind being thought of as Lady Luck, for they are,
quite often, as though the mystery of a Tarot deck."

THE CHILDREN BELIEVE SPRING

Voices outside the house fade into the mist,
as opposed to voices in the minds of the maddest.
Where shall the next voice come from:
The TV? The other side of the pond?
The vast stretches of sand with the voices
of waves hushing us as if we were babies?

Truly we must open a beer bottle for some
sort of voice. Its hiss encourages us
to drink even more. The father too tired
to rise from his easy chair: so he holds still.
The dog overexerts himself: a growl is what
he has to say. The window's light fades out.

The children become parents by playacting.
For they believe spring keeps its promises.

BESTIARY

The small triumph of a hummingbird.
A hyena pack's last laugh,
chasing off lions from a fresh kill.
A beauty contest winner: the peacock.
What, according to earthly measure,
is left that beasts have not already done?
Congratulations, butterfly, for your airy
spirit which makes us want to be like you.

Ah, elephants, headed for the zoo, let's hope
you are rewarded for all your grace.
In Africa, those with a price on your heads,
you walking tusks. Forgive the greedy.

POEM MEANT TO SATISFY HORACE'S *ARS POETICA* AS TO WHAT LITERATURE SHOULD DO

The wind cannot whistle, for it has no lips,
though it sounds like it's whistling, a strong wind,
as it turns the corners of houses or passes
between two buildings set close to each other.
And there is always room for a day
with its small kindnesses: a rose, an apple, a book
given to someone for her twenty-first birthday.
What true fabric we are made of! On good days
we delight at seeing the sun in a cloudless sky.
Days not so good, we are still able to make
a suitable breakfast, having gotten up earlier
than usual for whatever task requires more time.
Remain faithful to that which most pleases you.
Try to be as benevolent with things as a new mother.

THE BRILLIANCE
AND THE WISDOM

A brilliant joke might be like a poem
by Emily Dickinson: bite-sized.
And we see better hearing each.
Let's say a bracing wisdom honors both.
Let's say Emily is richer but less immediate.

Now the birds begin to trust us more.
They build nests in trees
just outside our doors.
It seems we are a risk worth taking,
especially for the grackles
that forage in our vicinity.

Yes, Emily's lines get shorter;
Whitman's longer. A great feeling
of transcendence comes over us
because of them—by night
we sleep in their auras.

THE CLOUDS OVER
TWO SMALLER SHAPES

In the distance of a city block,
out of earshot from me,
is it a mother
confronting her child?
He is maybe four or five.
She removes her hat,
holds it in her right hand.
She wipes her forehead.
He must look up—
to her face, to the clouds.

No oration on her part,
the idea is more like
the give-and-take
in Plato's dialogues, since
she speaks first, then he.

But a few exchanges later,
she drops her head.
And the boy makes a wry face,
which causes her to do the same.

Aha, their lips move simultaneously.
Who is listening less?
She doesn't pull him by the arm.
She doesn't shake him either.
Rather, she kisses his head.
He smiles. Now it's over.

CONCERT

I seek out the depths of the grand piano's shining.
It might very well be just a table with a keyboard
and some tightly strung wire, though its essence
transcends the earth. This black god makes
time bearable for pianist and audience alike.
No one can fathom its secrets which are infinite.
A singer without vocal cords, it exhales sound.
And it stands for nothing else but its own airy spirit.

YOUNG IN ACADIA PARISH

Should we stop thinking tomorrow will be better?
Maybe it won't. Maybe it'll be the same as today.
As for me, I can't stop thinking about childhood.
What was there to suggest the person I am now?
I see myself on my grandfather's tractor, a boy
who hit a fence, which cost Pa Pa money to fix.
He forgave me, but I took it hard. To this day
my first cousin reminds me of it while laughing.
I chased chickens. I ran the fields with dogs. I set
a wasps' nest on fire. I kicked crawfish mounds.
Summer and the sun makes me sweat, me just standing
there. To look for a shady tree is the best thing.
Then I help Pa Pa scatter corn for the Plymouth Rocks.
Milking the cow: another matter. Pa Pa lets me try,
though I can't get the timing of my hands just right.
"That's OK, *mon 'tit*, you can help gather eggs."
Later he slits a hog's throat and butchers it. Tonight
we'll eat pork chops, fresh, tasty, their fat ready to burn.

THE GHOSTS OF THE BOOKS IN THE LIBRARY

Restless. At two in the morning they hold forth.
There will never be anything like it,
how words stand at attention between covers.
Surely most of us walk the pages of books
as we walk through our lives—innocently.
But was Melville's white whale more than just
a whale? Was Hawthorne's guilt our own guilt?
Sundays the janitors don't come here.

THE OCTOGENARIAN
WHO STILL LIKES SINATRA

Muffled music from the apartment upstairs.
Frank Sinatra, I think. The renter still keeps
long-playing vinyl records and his stereo.
It is 2007. I can't begrudge him his nostalgia,
though I play CDs. How hard it is to keep up.
How space and time shift like tectonic plates.
The last great tsunami in the Indian Ocean
was so devastating I had to watch TV.
I had to see and see again a portent. Anyway,
we've got some breathing room. For now.
For now not even zebras show fear of lions.
(At least in the documentary I watch.)
Is our president a lion, not exactly brave, but one
who takes the lives of those too weak to fend?

BOYS, BEAUTY, RATTLESNAKES

Beauty that is the poisonous snake, I forgive you.
Since I was a boy, I have wanted to hold you,
yet not be bitten. Impossible? Maybe.
But in dreams everything is possible,
and so I wish not to be a boy again, where
snakes hide under my bed with alligators,
preventing me from climbing out into a new day
with its breakfast, its dressing, its school busses.
Before that the dawn of battles with colors.
Afterward, a bumpy ride to school where
Mrs. Giblin scolds us for not learning theorems.
You know: angles, parallelograms, circumferences.
Where would we be without the circle of the sun?
Where would we be without the moon, its own beauty?

FALSTAFF

There is no Shakespeare. He left with all
the others whose names fill the obituaries.
There is just Falstaff, on stage, denouncing honor.
Certainly no lack of wars, only gestures
toward stopping them, like dawn roosters, boastful,
self-centered, and when you get right down to it, afraid.

Tonight the Tigris and Euphrates flow free,
but I am unable to simply dip my hands in either.

ANDANTE

Some days you can almost imagine
how what Aristotle called "the good life"
could happen. After a gloomy week,
you would still love to smell flowers,
still love college football, dancing
in the rain, and when you are at last
no one, you would leave your body
quietly, content that you have loved
and been loved like a giant panda.
The key word has to be "loved" since
only thus has your life been set free.
You might even invoke the spirit of Eliot:
"To make an end is to make a beginning."
No claptrap here, folks. Why else does
the runner, full of heart, finish the race?

IV

FEBRUARY 14TH

Soon, but not until then, even after
the stars appear—so awfully many—that's when
I'll take my love and place it in a rose
which I'll place in your hand on Valentine's.
And even though February is a hard month,
I'll save times for outings to movies, to dances,
even to the museum where art will still astonish us,
for astonishment is never a paltry thing,
to be lightly passed over, as if it didn't
matter, for it does, between you and me,
our together astonishment, more beautiful
than skiing down a hill at full speed,
knowing ice, cold to the touch, not something
I'd wish for you, my lovely warm valentine.

12 DALTON ROAD

"It's angst!" he flew off the handle. "Shut up,"
she replied. Their marriage was that way:
one liners strung together like glass beads.
Were it not for the comical smile, one might
think him to be a washed-up actor still
with some brio, but no prospects for work.
Their living room centerpiece—an exact replica
of an alligator made somehow in plastic.
"Bite or be bitten," he would often say.
She concurred. What else could her hairdo mean?
Anybody's guess. Maybe they could have hired
a resident critic to tell of its symbolic effect.
When in a bookstore or a library he liked to put
his favorite books where only he could find them.
When at the beach, he liked to stand on his head.
It was said she was once a trapeze artist,
who had run away from the circus,
back home, instead of the other way around.
But pay attention to their cat: the real human being,
whose every step is patient and cautious.

WEDNESDAY ONLY
IN SOME OF OUR MINDS

One can't imagine not wearing blue jeans all
one's life, but it does become a problem when—
asked to be a pallbearer at a funeral, something
requiring a suit—you own none, are too broke
to buy one so you recommend another to take your place.
And funerals in the rain require the utmost forbearance.
Of course, rain doesn't matter to the dead, so there's
at least one person who couldn't care less.

Let's set matters crooked. The weather will be
there with or without you: consider it your friend.
Consider it a way to be entertained—wear the rain
alone in the woods after taking your clothes off.
No one will be hurt. Not even the squirrel cares,
but goes about its business of burying acorns like money.

In college (1968) I saw streakers dash from dorm
to dorm in the rain. Never arrested, they only
had warning letters written to their parents by the Dean.

It's late summer, and Wednesday in the minds
of everyone except those, who for one reason or other,
can't remember which day of the week it is.

THE COMPRESSED MATTER OF YOUTH

The girl dressed in long, stringy hair
and a purple woolen hat her mother knitted
has instructions imprinted in her mind.
They say: "Buy Mom a book recommended
by my best friend," also a teenager, but
she can't remember if it's in "Western Philosophy"
or "Psychology," one section in which her friend
pointed it out to her before. Half-awake, half
in reverie, she recalls neither author nor title.
Nada. Plan B calls for a walk in the park.
Grizzly old men. Some dogs pulling their owners.
A ball thrown against a wall. It returns.
What if the ball bounced from the atmosphere into space?
What if the rain began going upward? Such things
occurred to her. Assuming gravity reversed itself.
Ah, the ball is traveling far, back to her childhood.
That is why it doesn't matter that it's raining.

LIKE JUDY GARLAND, ONE OF THE GUMM SISTERS

People with stage names or pen names
or even the alias of a prizefighter:
Muhammad Ali for Cassius Clay.
They are never who we think they are,
always showing us different parts of themselves.
A handshake might mean good-bye, a wink, hello.
What are their daily lives like (nightly also)?
Is jazz essential to wake up to, like kisses?

Look. The sun is setting on Lupe Victoria Cortinas
whose real name is Beatrice Jimenez, whose father
couldn't drink beer in bars serving one color only.
She has stiffened to insult, has cast it aside.
Her novels take place in the barrios of El Paso.
Her sun is the best sun because of a good angle.
(When afraid she still makes the sign-of-the-cross.)
Given to her eyes, the light makes its peace.
Poised facing her head, the sun gives its blessing.

HAPPY BIRTHDAY

Laundry in the sky? I'm certain of it.
Certainly, dirty or clean laundry, the clouds.
Yes, the clothes of toddlers give their moms
lots to do as well. Think of them playing.
On tricycles. In backyard pools. In front of TV,
rolling around and impeccably adamant.
Carried, they live near the bodies of fathers.
On their knees they know the world below.
What can be known? Just who can know it?

To a child a happy face might mean an apology,
the best of which, however, involves cuddling.
With big eyes, open mouths, they are beyond us.
No apple can ever hide from them. Nor any kitten.
I would like, just once in my life, to stand
next to a three-year-old blowing out the candles,
all the others, too, in a microcosm of pleasure.

WHO ABETS WAR? WHO DOES NOT?

I'm late, but I've got
my whole life to make amends.
Think of it! A shrinking lifetime
which no one can store away
for later. More amazing:
that some people live
when they are supposed to die.
Don't mind me; I've not
cornered the market on mortality.
I can't complain about
my exile from New Orleans
because I'm among other exiles.
It's not political like Dante's.
More like my friend Farid's from Iran.
Just better to be among friends,
the likes of whom can be found
in any place we call home.

Yes, when the gods say war,
what is it you think we're stuck with?

IS HE STILL ALIVE?

The only sound: the wooden chair
creaking as I shift my weight.
Now I hear a drip from the faucet.
A dog barks once beyond my window.
Who else has known reading this quietly?
And reading makes me think: "How does
one say *phooey* in Spanish? Or Turkish?
How is the mind even capable of juggling
several languages together, polyglot?"
Does "come on by" have an equivalent?
In any language? I would think so. I would
not like to be left in a classroom without words.
But give me the country any day of the week.
How one's shoes get wet in the dew of morning!
How as a child I took pleasure in chasing chickens!
No city boy really, still I lived in the city
most of the year. Summers meant being
with my grandparents on 25 acres of farm.
They meant walking to the barn
with Grandfather whose favorite show was "Gunsmoke."
Ah, James Arness. A cowboy with tact,
a lawman. Is he still alive? I don't think so.

HE WHO LEAVES HIS MONEY IN MUTUAL FUNDS

The pines fit nicely among each other.
An oil company leased this land, but no oil.
Evangeline Parish. Grandfather to father
to son. The timber alone keeps it worthwhile.

But the son lives nowhere near the pines.
In his life are stoplights, large grocery stores,
sidewalks, beggars, a downtown. How public!
It'd be easy to say he had no good friends.
Co-workers instead. Who, over the years, have
made him less selfish, more sympathetic.
He sees. Wintertime as being invincible.
For it's already no one's little darling.
This morning he snapped the swords of ice
hanging from his bumper. Sucked on one
like a popsicle. No, these simple maneuvers
won't get him elected president, whom
even his mother didn't want him to become.
"Become a shoe salesman," she told him
on his eighteenth birthday without cake
or ice cream. He considered. So he did.

FOR DANIEL

Ah, which me is this me
I'm inhabiting, serious yet playful?
Am I *homo ludens*, the man of games?
I like to get into wrestling matches
with my nephew who is ten.
That way I can make him laugh.
His hair: blond as mine was
back when. Already he is
beginning to understand science.
"Did you know," I asked him,
"that the ice in the glass is
not really making the water cold,
but in fact is absorbing heat?"
"I know," he said, "Dad told me."
"Good for you," I said, admiring
the light his eyes reflect.

Young and promising child:
I am solving love as I would
an equation. The answer is all of us.

PREREQUISITES

Homer Horton, known as Uncle Bob,
took me aside in the butcher shop

and said: "If you go to med school,
you'll be glad you learned how to cut up

a side of beef. Of course, you'll have to take
your Latin and your Greek." He was 65 in '65

when he told me this. He didn't know
they weren't prerequisites any more.

Nor did I tell him he needed to update
his mental maps like a keen geographer.

He sometimes bickered with the other butchers.
But he was excellent with customers.

From the freezer I once brought him an oxtail
because I had no clue what it was. So I asked.

"Oh that," he said. "That there's a flyswatter."

www.ingramcontent.com/pod-product-compliance
Lightning Source LLC
Chambersburg PA
CBHW021023090426
42738CB00007B/886